About the Author

John Carter was born in north Wiltshire in 1952. He has always had a fascination with humorous illustrations, possibly stemming from early visits to the dentist and looking through *Punch Magazine*. A great admirer of the illustrators, Edward Lear and George Cruikshank, John has developed his own style over the years. In this first collection of *Absolute Stuff 'n' Nonsense*, John has created a cast of imaginary characters poking fun at everyday life and events through rhyme and illustration. John continues to write and draw, dividing his time between Wiltshire and the Limousin region of France.

Absolute Stuff'n'Nonsense

VANGUARD PRESS PAPERBACK

© Copyright 2021
John Carter

A CIP catalogue record for this title is
available from the British Library.
ISBN 978-1-80016-031-6

*Vanguard Press is an imprint of
Pegasus Elliot MacKenzie Publishers Ltd.
www.pegasuspublishers.com*

First Published in 2021

**Vanguard Press
Sheraton House Castle Park
Cambridge England**

Printed & Bound in Great Britain

John Carter

Absolute Stuff'n'Nonsense

Vanguard Press

A Book of Utter Twaddle

Dear readers, to this book please adhere,
For the verse that you read will, I fear,
Cause the classical brain
To go mad and insane,
With an apology to one Edward Lear.

Kibble Popkin grew a beard
That reached beyond his chin.
He walked each day to John O'Groats,
And then walked back-a-gin.

A gentleman angler of note,
On perceiving a fish while afloat.
Categorically denied
And denounced that its size
Was somewhat at odds with his boat.

The Right Reverend Archibald Pug,
Observed on his nose a large bug.
When asked, "What's its size?"
He ecclesiastically replied,
"Well it's certainly not a small grub."

A friend said, "Why have you sat,
in a chair wearing such a large hat?

"It is obvious to me
That all I can see,
Is your tummy all bloated and fat."

"I have eaten far too much of the pud,
On its arrival looked ever so good.

"So, I sit here and wait for my tum to deflate,
Under heavy disguise of this hood."

In an olive grove on the island of Crete,
Lived a man who pressed fruit with his feet.
When they turned bruised and sore
From the olive's stone core.
He would stop and then rest on the beach.

On a fence I observed a small bird,
In the spring on April the third.
By the fourth it had gone,
Taking with it its song.
Now I wait feeling sadly perturbed.

An aristocratic lady of Kent,
On finding a penny all bent.
Remarked on her find, that luck was unkind.
As it was required to be urgently spent.

Several young men came to gloat,
On observing an old man with a goat.
"What a sad looking thing," said one with a sting,
"Its condition is worse than my coat."
Said the other, with a sound of intent,
"It smells and could be incontinent."
With its patches of bald, it must so old,
Why its legs are all twisted and bent."
The old man said, "Why do you jest?
For I fear that the goat will do best.
He does not amuse and has a short fuse."
Then the goat with a kick did the rest.

A lady from Cheltenham Spa,
Whose snobbery surpassed many by far.
Was caught drinking beer, from a bottle, I fear.
Whilst doing the splits on the bar.

A chef from Kent took a look,
On receiving by post a thick book.
Swiftly turning its pages that didn't take ages.
She announced, "In here, there's nothing to cook.

A noble young lady with wealth,
At auction one day bought some Delft.
Whilst carrying it back home, she tripped on a stone.
Causing some slight distress and ill health.

The Nob of Screwed,
thus, spake his men,
Was such a noble man.
So brave was he that all could see,
From Norway to Nanchang.

The Nob of Screwed,
Lived in a tower perched high
upon a crag.
That all below looked up to him
And none of them were sad.

The Nob of Screwed,
He served them food of rats' tails string and cheese,
And afterwards washed down with oil,
He gave them boiled bees.

The Nob of Screwed,
Was eight feet tall and wore a golden crown,
He dressed in mail from head to foot,
That weighed the poor man down.

So now at last his time had come
No more for him to see.
The Nob of Screwed,
Has passed away, and all lived happily.

Wilfred Snook met a cat while walking into town.
Said Wilfred Snook to the cat,
"Why mope and look so down?"
The cat replied, "It's very sad you
find me not in clover."
"But tell me where do fishes go,
when the river's frozen over?"

I walked into a bar one day
And pondered on a drink.
The barman asked,
"What's your pleasure, sir?"
I said, "Just let me think."
I looked at all the options
And something that I'd like.
"Surprise with your speciality."
So, he rode his one wheeled bike.

How strange and odd can life be,
On observing a young elephant in a tree.
When I asked, "Do you climb?"
He shakenly replied,
"How I got here is a mystery to me."

Down by the water a crocodile
was looking intensely at me.
Assuming I was something to munch on,
A tasty morsel to have for its tea.
It stealthily crept out of the water and
approached me as quiet as a mouse.
Whereupon I turned around and whacked it,
landing a punch right upon its wide mouth.
"Don't you realise what I am?" I said forcefully.
With my foot pressing down on its head.
"Elephants are creatures not to mess with,
I'm playing otherwise you'd be dead."

An elderly lady of Rhyl,
Asked the doctor to prescribe her a pill.
To cure colds and coughs,
And dismiss all her spots.
So, she could comfortably stroll around Rhyl.

Said a milkmaid from Paddington Green,
Who for weeks no cows she had seen?
"It is totally absurd in this place is no herd."
So, she left and now lives in Brean.

You sit and with gentle persuasion,
The rumbling inside your inside
Develops into wild devastation,
Then hopefully stand up with pride.

The host said, "It's just as I feared,
The man over there with a beard.
Is so heavily disguised,
that not even his eyes
can be seen clearly through his thick beard."

The doctor said, "Sorry I'm late,
The traffic is bad, which I hate."
He then picked up the cat,
Gave a pat to its back.
"Does your child often get in this state?"

A middle-aged lady from Ongar,
Requested a dress slightly longer.
As the thing's far too short,
The fabric's too taut
And the next one had better be stronger.

A lady from West Zanzibar,
Purchased a left-hand drive car.
She drove to the east
Met a one-legged priest,
Then drove back to West Zanzibar.

A rather posh lady of Corinium,
Requested two bottles, both with gin in 'em.
The first she drank quick,
The second, downed in a sip.
Before throwing out the empties
And binning 'em.

You've had the starter, now the main,
The pudding's just a breeze.
You're feeling stuffed, so just break wind.
Now there's room for cheese.

A man fell into a large pot,
At the time was exceedingly hot.
He stayed for a week to warm up his feet.
As they were the only two, that he'd got.

Whilst walking my dog through Mayfair,
My eyes came transfixed on a hare.
Dressed in waistcoat bowtie, it's no word of a lie.
For it positively made me stare.

A gentleman on perceiving a swan,
Observed with the bird something wrong.
"This may sound absurd, that I feel most perturbed.
But do swans wear top hats and sing songs?"

In a boat, out rowing one day,
On a lake in the middle of May.
Said one to another,
"We had better call mother,
As disaster is pending, I'd say."

Today is Friday and it's wet,
The past week's been the same.
In fact, this month has been quite damp,
It's driving me insane.
As one day follows another,
The rain just pours straight down.
I feel another day like this
And all the trees may drown.

A lady, the Duchess of Pratt,
Observed in a shop a large hat.
She said for a sonnet
I'll purchase that bonnet,
As it rather resembles my cat.

Balth and Casp, were two wise men,
Who lived beyond the sea.
They never came or never went,
Because they'd lost the key.

An old man sold me a carrot,
He said, "That's the biggest you'll see."
When I said, "No it ain't."
He said, "File your complaint,
With the lady who sold it to me."

A dog by the name of Woodbark,
Took a ride into town on a cart.
Where he danced by the light
Of the streetlamps at night.
Before being whisked off, by a tart.

I sit upon this stool and look
upon a so-called friend.
I sit and ponder thoughts so deep,
they drive me round the bend.
Oh, why oh why one such as me
should have a friend like that,
When I'm a timid little mouse
and he's a ruddy cat.

Two cats named Kitty and Puss,
Into town they both travelled by bus.
Where they sat upon silk
And dined upon milk,
Before riding back home in the bus.

"What a nice day we're having tomorrow,"
Said the station master talking in song.
"I feel happy and all full of sorrow.
Because the next train to arrive has just gone."

A vicar out flying a kite,
With his son, when it disappeared from sight.
"Why heavens, where's it gone?"
Said the worried young son.
"Have no fear, it's attached to your bike."

To sit beside a wandering brook,
A river or a stream.
A boat upon the lake or sea,
Is every fisherman's dream.
By day or night in sun or rain,
No matter what the day.
And then back home to brag and boast,
Of the one that got away.

When listening to opera,
One thing springs to mind.
A somewhat large vocalist,
With an imposing behind.
Producing a sound very few could repeat,
To an operatic partner, insipid and weak.
From prelude to aria then recitative,
Where the Don gets his sword
tangled up in his sleeve.
Then right at the end of this display with surprise.
Our heroine belts a song out,
coughs loudly then dies.

There was an old man who lived up a pole,
When a stranger asked, "Why, sir, when the wind is so cold?"
"I find it quite bracing to sit here and stare,
Watch the world pass by slowly, with not even a care.
All my food is brought daily, as well as good wine.
Will you come up and join me? As I'm ready to dine.
There are good days and bad days, but what I will say,
Hold on rather tightly, as today is May Day."

Ups and downs and on and offs,
Smutty banter can be quirky.
With humour at its lowest ebb.
"That joke you told was dirty."

It happened so very quickly,
While waiting for a bus in the Strand.
I waved down the conveyance most politely,
Whereupon it trimmed all the nails on my hand.

There were two old men who lived in a bin,
One very large and the other rather thin.
They lived upon leaves, pine nuts and wild rice,
Accompanied by lashings of Cornish vanilla ice.
The one who was fat had friends round for dinner.
So, the one who was thin had to fast to get thinner.
So, the moral of this tale, when entertaining in a bin.
Get it emptied twice weekly, before others move in.

Golf, some may say, is a sensible game,
A pleasant country walk, in sunshine or rain.
Continuously bashing a small ball around,
While attempting eighteen times,
to send it to ground.
Now others may have a different opinion.
Defacing natural countryside,
for man's artificial dominion.
Digging countless small holes
and building sand beaches.
Furthermore, thwarting most
of nature's wild species.
So, appeasing both sides of a sensitive dilemma,
Plant trees, so the world can
revive and breathe better.

A young man holding a goat,
When the chain round its neck simply broke.
He said, "This demise,
Leaves me almost surprised,
As it takes most the strain from its throat."

While walking my dog down a long muddy lane,
I met with this gal called Lady Ghislaine.
With two dogs sauntering by, both soggy and black,
And she in a raincoat plus large floppy hat.
"Do you walk here each day?" I asked most politely.
Her answer was, "yes, but slow, never sprightly."
What a charming young lady, I thought as we parted.
Then she tripped, yelled out, "Fluck!"
fell flat and then farted.

I know that I'm a smart dressed chap,
Although my friends do sneer.
My teeth, my own, are pearly white,
My eyes are bright and clear.
My feet are on the larger size,
For me, they're not to blame.
My hands are just a little small,
My tum puts me to shame.

When I was young, a little chap,
My tum was not this size.
But as I grew from year to year,
This thing I just despised.
As boyhood turned to manhood,
And soft drinks turned to beer.
With gradual bulging of my tum,
Attributions disappeared.

My history left behind me,
Reflection on years past.
My teeth are not so pearly white,
My eyes a mist is cast.
Although my tum juts out a mile
And both feet disappear.
One thing I still enjoy the most,
Is all that lovely beer.

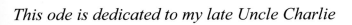

This ode is dedicated to my late Uncle Charlie

A gent while out riding his bike,
Observed several girls on a hike.
"It appears that your walk,
Has caused some distraught.
I sense that your boots are too tight."

Said the girl to the gent, "You are right,
For my pair were so cheap for their type.
And my friend here's the same,
But they have a posh name."
"You've been sold ruddy fakes, what a gripe."

"So, when buying named goods on the street,
Make certain you request a receipt.
For if you're walking about
And long distance, no doubt.
There's nothing so bad as sore feet."

Drinking water is so terribly mundane,
You could suffer H2O on the brain.
The result from this tipple,
The spoken word becomes drivel.
Just in case pour the stuff down the drain.

Now wine is a drink with all frills,
Its bouquet will enhance the nostrils.
In its taste you will savour,
Versatility of flavour.
It could cure you from ailments and ills.

Some say water is good for your wits,
Where wine, mental faculties end in bits.
Then water dilutes,
Few say wine it pollutes.
But have you ever quaffed water for kicks?

Most experts will tell you, the way to define,
An extraction from the grape, is the way to make wine.
No other concoctions made from spuds and the like,
Elderberries and parsnip, would give experts a fright.
Wine should be tasted with friends not alone.
From France, Bordeaux, Burgundy, Loire and the Rhone. Germany's finest from Moselle to the Rhine,
From Portugal, Italy, and Spain are all fine.

Also new world discoveries, their wines we can savour,
Producing such vintage with wonderful flavour.
You sit and relax, pop a cork, toast good cheer,
For the wine you are drinking comes from the home
of warm beer.

Gobby Cobbler picked his nose from morning,
noon to night.
He picked and flicked at everything,
which made the cat take fright.
Gobby Cobbler's nose grew large
through all its constant picking.
His mother said, "Son, don't do that,
especially in the kitchen."
But Gobby took no notice,
of doctors, friends and kin.
Then one day he picked his last,
because his head caved in.

Tommy Gunter rode into
town upon a cart all battered.
On their return the horse collapsed,
it too was feeling knackered.
Tommy Gunter rode his bike
because the horse had snuffed it.
On his return, cycling up a hill,
poor old Tommy huffed it.
Tommy Gunter, sat in his chair,
feet up and feeling tired.
On his return, he'd not felt well,
then Tommy just expired.

The boy stood on the burning deck, in hand a map of Cuba. While down below the captain played a tune upon his tuba.

The captain said, "What's this a-foot?"
The boy said, "Just an ankle."
"Then let out all the fishing nets."
Whereupon they came entangled.

The boy he yelled, "There's land ahead,
Just row a little longer."
But the more they tried, the less it went,
For the wind was getting stronger.

By now it seems, this ditty's gone,
a mighty long way off course.
It's turned into a load of junk,
Just like a Chinese seahorse.

The boy stood on the burning deck,
The sun was shining brightly.
Not far away a
golden beach,
"Stay here, not
bloody likely."

The Flart is a creature that lives in a den,
It creeps out at night, then creeps back again.
It eerily moans in the deadest of night,
Sending chills down your spine,
that will make you take fright.
The Flart with its speed can move very fast.
One second, it's with you and the next it has passed.
The Flart it is devilish for the tricks it will play,
And there's nothing to stop it, or keep it at bay.
So, remember at night,
keep your doors tightly locked.
All your windows and chimneys,
keep shut and keep blocked.
So, this fiendish young devil is kept well away.
For some other poor victim, is the Flart's easy prey.

The Ibblecombe Dibblecombe Tabblecombe spot,
Is something that is found on your toes.

The Ibblecombe Dibblecombe Tabblecombe spot,
May also appear on your nose.

The Ibblecombe Dibblecombe Tabblecombe spot,
Appears completely by chance.
When you cough or you sneeze, or get caught in a breeze.
It will either be there or be not.

The Ibblecombe Dibblecombe Tabblecombe spot,
Can blow itself up like a ball.
Appear twice the size, on your ears or your eyes,
Or never appear at all.

For the Ibblecombe Dibblecombe Tabblecombe spot,
In error you think it's the pox.
For the pox, no it ain't, so don't weaken or faint,
When they pop like a jack-in-the-box.

A prudent young doctor of Bath,
Was approached by a man in a mask.
Hiding a number of bruises and cuts,
Down the front of his face and way passed his guts.
The scar it continued way over his tum,
Turned right by his knee, back up to his bum.
Then straight up his back and under his arm.
The accident had happened in a field on his farm.
The doctor said firstly "We'll just clean you up,
For the mask you are wearing is only some muck."
A nurse gently tittered, his wife gave a laugh.
But the farmer on moving, fell completely in half.

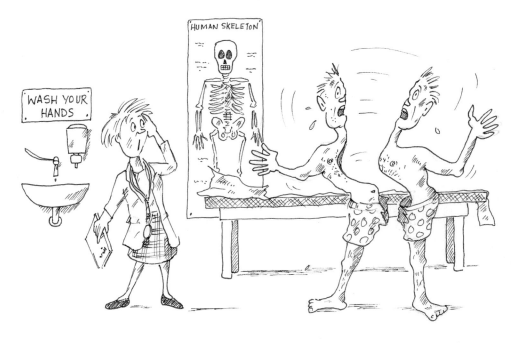

The Garvakovar is a creature,
That good-hearted people should fear.
The Garvakovar is so hideous,
That you'll not want this thing to appear.

Its gaze, like a swift bolt of lightning,
Will reduce the onlooker to dust.
Its appearance is so dreadfully frightening.
And its odour, is one of disgust.

So, if you're out on your own at the twilight,
And you hear a strange sound at your heel.
With the stench of corruption in your nostrils.
Then the Garvakovar is quite near.

In a land not far from Nepal,
Where pigs and cabbages grow tall.
Lives an odd-looking chap,
But a wisely old sap,
Whose stone house resembles a ball.

He travels each day on a wheel,
That's propelled by a left flippered seal.
From his home in the hills,
Where he lives upon pills.
Which give him both pep and great zeal.

He is ageless and never looks drawn,
He was old on the day he was born.
But his army of cats, and air force of bats,
Patrol his land that's no boundary or bourn.

If you ask him the time, he'll just strut,
While drinking cold cabbage juice from a cup.
Sing you songs, tell great tales,
Of how he once lived in Wales.
That's the Great Nob of Hillabar-Hut.

The Gollocock bird looks exceedingly absurd,
If you think it resembles a crow.
But the Gollocock bird however observed,
And whatsoever you think who you know.

The Gollocock bird is not what you think,
For a fact it resembles no other.
The Gollocock bird, not feeling perturbed,
Does not even resemble its brother.

The Gollocock bird not feeling demure,
Will never resemble a hen.
For a hen is obese, to say but the least,
And a fine hearty feast for another.

The Gollocock bird with its wings so small,
Would never attempt to fly.
For try as it may, on terra firma it'll stay,
It's often seen with a tear in its eye.

The Gollocock bird has plumage so fine,
Encasing its body so thin.
When you tickle its toes,
Or comment on its clothes.
It will puff out its chest like a king.

For the origination of such a creation,
Is itself what man thinks absurd.
But it's not what you think,
Or where is that link,
For it's only the Gollocock bird.

The Gollacock bird

SNIFFER

Hiccup, Tizzard and Bile, were the best solicitors
around.
They took all the briefs, from all the top thieves,
To prevent them from being sent down.

When a little-known felon named Sniffer,
Decided to pull off a job.
He sussed out the joint, worked out every point,
And made certain they hadn't a dog.

Sniffer had made sure that this evening,
That no one was to be around.
The night it was still and no sign of old bill.
So, he crept in, without making a sound.

He broke in through the lavatory window,
Then worked his way right through the house.
He filled up his bag, which professionals call swag,
And attempted to leave like a mouse.

Now Sniffer was not a smart fella,
And as most skilful burglars will know.
When you enter a joint, you make of the point,
You leave by the self-same window.

First of all, out
went the lolly,
Then Sniffer jumped
out with no sound.
But his top made a loop,
which caught on a hook.
Poor Sniffer was a long
way from ground.

He had jumped out the upstairs window,
A rather long way from the deck.
Not a sound did he make, nor movement or quake.
For the fear of breaking his neck.

While hanging around like a parrot,
Not even attempting to fly.
This sound it was heard by an inquisitive bird,
A policeman, who was just passing by.

In a language understood by no other,
 The policeman said, "What's all this here?"
Then from up in the sky, came Sniffer's reply.
"I only called round for a beer."

The evidence was right there before him,
Sniffer was sent down for trial.
He did not stand a chance as the magistrate did glance.
But defending was old Mister Bile.

"Sir," said the eminent lawyer.
"Before you stands this pitiful young man.
However, he tries." Then with tears in his eyes,
Continued with all of his sham.

The magistrate pondered all matters,
Told the court that all crime must be kicked.
"And the lawyer your patter did not really matter.
As it was my house your client had picked."

Daphne Poke went down a well,
To see if there was water.
When she emerged,
Her feet were wet
So were the shoes, her mother bought her.

Christmas has gone for another long year,
The new year's next, that involves drinking more beer.
Eating more food and stuffing one's face.
Then acting quite stupid,
What an utter disgrace.

Stan and Ed were two young boys,
Who every day, played with their toys.
With utter devotion they played together,
Broad happy smiles and anger, never.
As they grew into adulthood,
Their toys they played, as much as could.

So now they're old and still they play,
Not quite so much, like every day.
But then one day poor Stanley died,
Ed shed a tear and nearly cried.
"It's definitely a sad old day,
and at last I can throw those toys away."

Chop and Stick, sat down to lunch,
And dine upon fried rice.
Said Chop to Stick, "This food is good, in fact it's
very nice."
"Just one problem," said Stick to Chop,
We only have one pair."
"We'll take in turns to eat our rice,
As not to cause despair."

This planet that we live on, some say, is in a state.
This planet that we live on, is a grave cause for debate.
It's taken many, years for mankind to reflect,
But now it's had that wake-up call, before it's totally wrecked.
Some call it global warming and others climate change.
There's those that call it nonsense and others just deranged.
But to look at this historically and what has gone before,
It started as a lump of rock, from surface to the core.
The planet cooled and growth began, with plants and moss and trees,
While creatures living in the drink,
Emerged from all the seas.
We then edge through some million years, when dinosaurs ruled the earth.
They hung around for quite some time,
But still no human birth.
It takes another age or so for Homo sapiens to make a show,
Eventually leaving a ruddy mess, as across the globe they flow.

So now to end this story and reflect upon Earth's plight.

We humans have made a nasty mess and not a pretty sight.

We're looking at extinction, of nearly every living thing.

We treat this planet recklessly, like an over full waste bin.

But we do like a happy ending, after trudging through this grot.

With flora and fauna all wiped out,

What's left is that lump of rock.

Sidney Tote, he liked a smoke,
As well as Mother's cooking.
He liked to smoke between each bite,
When mother wasn't looking.
Then one day he smoked his last,
Said, "Mom, I'm feeling tired."
He then slumped down in Dad's old chair,
Poor Sidney just expired.

Mom turned around while making rice pudding and
said, "I always said them fags would kill him."

Bonnie Fetter had a friend,
Who was good at making butter.
She tried to teach poor Bonnie this,
But sadly, had a stutter.

Up and down and down and up,
That's what steps are there for.
So, when you're down and not quite up,
You'll definitely need to climb more.

Mixing flour with eggs and milk,
Until the mixture's smooth as silk.
In the pan with butter, hot,
Spoon in the batter, just a drop.
Wait until one side is cooked,
To check, just peek and have a look.
Then toss the pancake in the air,
To cook its other side, still bare.
Hoping it lands back in the pan,
Not stuck to ceiling, as sometimes can.
The finished product, looking nice,
Serve up with sugar and a lemon slice.

This is the story of Ollie Glos, Old Spot,
Who liked warm and wet weather, But never too hot.
He scratched upon gate posts,
He scratched on his door.
When feeling contented, Ollie still scratched lots more.
In warm and wet weather, he would wallow in mud,
Ollie's mother had told him,
It was good for his blood.
At the end of the day when all scratching was done,
With no more mud bathing and contented full tum.
On a bed of fresh straw, Ollie would lay down to sleep,
And dream of more scratching, wallowing in mud nice and deep.

Billy Bennet bought a bike
And cycled out of town.
He cycled up a long steep hill
And then he freewheeled down.

Billy Bennet rode each day,
And miles to see his mum.
But all this riding caused distress,
Billy developed a sore red bum.

So, Billy Bennet changed his pants
Then filled them full of stuffing,
And now he rides more comfortably,
Even though he looks a muffin.

Henry Nutter had a stutter,
His wife was hard of hearing.
They'd lived together for sixty years,
Their time, just disappearing.

Every day was just the same,
Their routine never changed.
They'd take in turns to cook and clean,
With an occasional kiss exchanged.

Then one day they both dropped dead,
A neighbour said, "It's their age."
"And did you know," another said,
"They never spoke the same language."

The goat and the crow went out,
To look at the beautiful moon.
They gazed at the sky,
Reaching ever so high.
A dilemma ensued; it was noon.

The moon looked down at the goat and crow,
And asked them to make a wish.
They smiled at each other,
Then heartily laughed.
An opportunity they both couldn't miss.

The goat and the crow looked up at the moon,
In the middle of night.
It wasn't the moon shining bright in the sky,
But the Earth, what a wondrous sight.

Nick and Nock and brother Nosh,
Out in the country walking,
They walked from here and then to there,
While endlessly squawking and gawking.

"Time for bed," Mother said.
"Time to turn off social media."
 "But do we have to?"
"Yes, you do.
"Because I'm the one who feeds-ya."

"You wouldn't really starve us, Mom?"
"We love your tasty cooking."
"So, turn those things off, then to bed,
Because Dad's not had his pudding."

Potalot and Lotapot,
Were two good looking guys.
They ate a lot and drank a lot,
And both liked hot mince pies.

When Lotapot had drank a lot, Potalot asked him,
why?
So, Lotapot told Potalot,
His mother had just died.

Potalot and Lotapot
Embraced and kissed each other.
Then Potalot asked Lotapot,
"Move in, if there's no other."

So, Lotapot and Potalot,
Lived happily side by side.
They're like a married couple,
And both still like mince pies.

The Tickit-Tackit-Tockit bird,
Flew in from snowy climes.
To dine on quince and bags of mints,
While listening to nonsense rhymes.

He stayed a week, chatting with friends,
Reminiscing on years gone by.
And when the mints and quince had gone,
Up into the sky he'd fly.

The dim-witted Dick of Dunbar,
Arrived home late in his car.
Chauffeured erratically by his man,
Called one-eyed stuffed Sam.
To their home in western Dunbar.

A yawning horse and a yawning dog,
Were rudely awoken from sleep.
They'd slept all night by candlelight,
In the shadow of a Norman keep.

"What was that?" said the horse,
On hearing a noise, that the dog had heard before.
"It's the master upstairs flushing the loo, Out the
way! Before the crap hits the floor."

I've been outside,
My, my it's wet,
Earth's risen to meet the sky.
The water's rising, now knee deep,
Soon the fish will learn to fly.

Bonnie Fetter wrote a letter,
To the House of Lords.
Writing oh-so eloquently
And in not too many words.

My Lords, I thank you for your offer,
To join your noble throng,
But I'm a vegetarian,
So, wearing ermine is quite wrong.

With pipe in hand he made his mark,
to rid the town of rats.
While looking on and drinking cream,
were fat and lazy cats.
The townsfolk made a song and dance,
rejoicing at his feat.
But declined to pay the sum agreed,
upon his bill to meet.
The piper then he changed his tune,
and played a mellow song,
Then looking at the townsfolk said,
"Only once you'll do me wrong."
The music wafted through the air
and caught the children's ear.
Whereupon they all joined hands,
with laughter, joy and cheer.
Elders frozen to the spot,
while children danced in line
And made their way throughout the town,
to the piper's haunting chime.
They marched out into countryside,
beneath the city gate.

All smiled and sang and laughed and cheered,
not knowing what their fate.
Through golden fields of corn and wheat,
Children made their merry dance.
Meadows high with wavering grass,
all followed in a trance.
Ahead appeared a towering crag,
that reached towards the sky.
The piper stopped and pitched his tune,
with notes all soaring high.
A mighty crack as cannon fire, a roar and rush of air,
A door appeared within the rock
and all the children stared.
Mesmerised by an enchanting sound,
of piper's captive song,
All entered into nothingness,
a hypnotic and happy throng.
When all had passed the threshold,
safely ensconced inside.
The portal closed behind them
and ceased that living tide.
A lame and lonely mite was he,
his appearance not the same.
Tried desperately to follow,
but sadly all in vain.
Upon the rock he looked and stared,
where the happy throng had gone.
When sadness overwhelmed him,
his sun no longer shone.

All hope of seeing friends again,
he journeyed back so late,
And imparting news to those back home,
of all the children's fate.
Days and weeks and months passed by;
the town sank into sorrow.
Its young folk never would come home,
to return upon the morrow.
So, what of all the children,
who followed piper's call?
Not one of them was ever found,
when devoured by the wall.
And sadly, now to end this
tale of woeful grisly loss,
The sad and crippled beggar boy
hung himself from the town's high cross.
No pain he feels, now hanging there,
in a better place is he.
And children who the piper led,
play in paradise, where all are free.

Bonnie Fetter walking home,
Wondered what to have for supper.
She walked into a well-known store
And bumped into her brother.
"I can't think what to eat tonight,
I'm totally bored with pasta."
"I came in just for bread and milk,
As my cooking's a disaster."
They racked their brains on what to eat,
But neither could decide.
"The pub's next door, let's have a drink
And let their menu be our guide."

I drove one day to Leicester,
And then returned to Bicester.
I'd left my hat in Worcester,
So, I went via Cirencester.

On my way back home from Worcester,
I had a drink in Gloucester.
Then back through Cirencester,
And finally, home to Bicester.

Nellie Locket had a dog,
She also had a bear.
One day while walking in the street,
A nosey person stared.
"You know it's rude to stop and stare,
At someone you don't know?"
"Sorry," said the stranger.
"I thought that bear was Aunty Flo."

When I was young, my mother said,
"Don't forget to clean your teeth."
Up and down and round and round,
Especially the gums beneath.

So, each and every morning,
With brush in hand I'd clean.
And every night before my bed,
I'd make my teeth all gleam.

All through my life and without fail,
I'd perform my daily task.
And now I'm getting on a bit,
This chore's a mighty ask.

So, now I'm in my twilight years,
Most worries are long dead.
And the nicest thing about my teeth,
They're in a glass beside my bed.

A sweep by the name of Flue Sam,
Got his brush tightly caught in a jam.
With pushing and pulling to extract from this fix,
All he retrieved were some dirty old bricks.

Bottoms up and bottoms down,
This glass is nearly empty.
Fill them up, another round,
Make sure they're full and plenty.

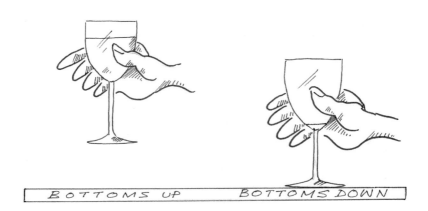

BOTTOMS UP   BOTTOMS DOWN

I sat on a bench admiring the view,
When a bird came and sat down beside.
What a brave little thing, I thought to myself,
It's observing all around in its stride.

It fluttered its wings then whistled a song,
Before soaring way up in the sky.
And as I looked up to wave my farewell,
The bugger dropped a gift in my eye.

Kibble Popkin wore a hat,
The size of an umbrella.
He wore it each and every day,
Making him a happy fella.

Kibble Popkin liked a dram,
Down at the local bar.
A liquid like an angel's kiss,
Known locally as uisge na beatha*.

In John-O-Groats he'd doff his hat,
Such a gentleman was he.
He then walked home to Back-A-Gin,
Just in time for tea.

*_Uisge na beatha_ Water of life, Scottish Gaelic,
pronounced, ush-ge-bah